Presented to:

Never Forget The Difference You've Made

Made in the USA
Las Vegas, NV
22 September 2023

77985007R00061